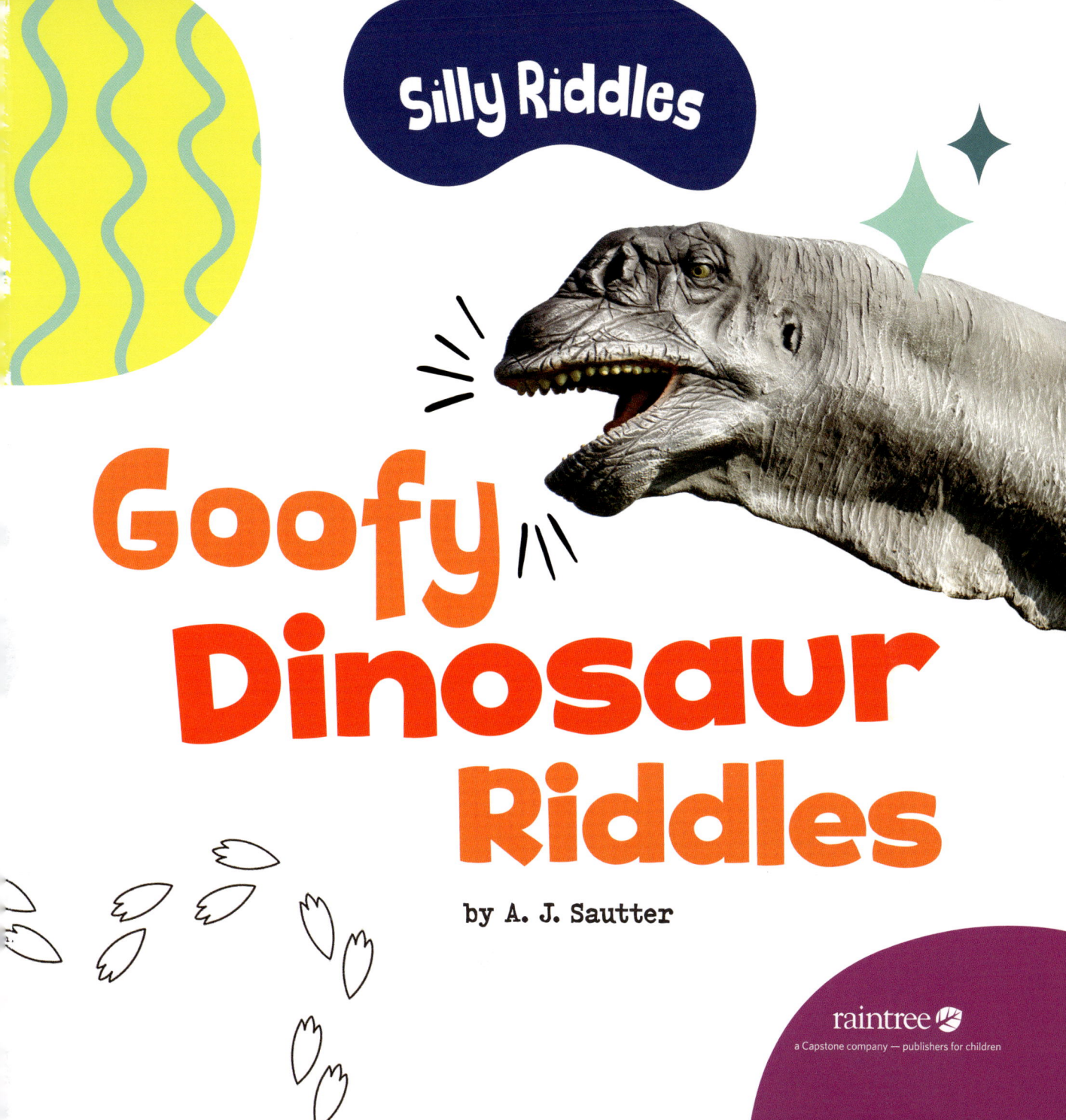

Silly Riddles

Goofy Dinosaur Riddles

by A. J. Sautter

raintree
a Capstone company — publishers for children

Raintree is an imprint of Capstone Global Library Limited, a company incorporated in England and Wales having its registered office at 264 Banbury Road, Oxford, OX2 7DY – Registered company number: 6695582

www.raintree.co.uk
myorders@raintree.co.uk

Hardback edition text © Capstone Global Library Limited 2024
Paperback edition text © Capstone Global Library Limited 2025

The moral rights of the proprietor have been asserted. All rights reserved. No part of this publication may be reproduced in any form or by any means (including photocopying or storing it in any medium by electronic means and whether or not transiently or incidentally to some other use of this publication) without the written permission of the copyright owner, except in accordance with the provisions of the Copyright, Designs and Patents Act 1988 or under the terms of a licence issued by the Copyright Licensing Agency, 5th Floor, Shackleton House, 4 Battle Bridge Lane, London, SE1 2HX (www.cla.co.uk). Applications for the copyright owner's written permission should be addressed to the publisher.

ISBN 978 1 3982 5408 4 (hardback)
ISBN 978 1 3982 5413 8 (paperback)

Editorial Credits
Editor: Aaron Sautter; Designer: Jaime Willems; Media Researcher: Rebekah Hubstenberger; Production Specialist: Whitney Schaefer

Photo Credits
Getty Images: breckeni, 16 (right), Dorling Kindersley, 9, Racksuz, 21, SCIEPRO, 10 (bottom right), SEBASTIAN KAULITZKI/SCIENCE PHOTO LIBRARY, 6, 10 (left, middle right), 12 (top right), 14 (middle), SEBASTIAN KAULITZKI/SCIENCE PHOTO LIBRARY, 15; Shutterstock: colnihko, design element (colour eye), GraphicsRF.com, 7 (middle), Hedzun Vasyl, cover (bottom left), 18, 19, kamomeen, 7 (top), 17, Marques, 8, metha1819, 11, NATALIA61, design element (googly eye), Noiel, cover (top right), 1 (top right), 20, oksanka007, design element (paper cutouts), Perfectorius, design element (symbols), StockArtRoom, design element (shapes), Suwat wongkham, 4, Ton Bangkeaw, 13, YuRi Photolife, 5

British Library Cataloguing in Publication Data
A full catalogue record for this book is available from the British Library.

Printed and bound in India.

Contents

Prehistoric puzzlers 4
Super stumpers 10
Baffling brainteasers 16
    Glossary 22
    Find out more 23
    Index 24
    About the author 24

Words in **bold** are in the glossary.

Prehistoric puzzlers

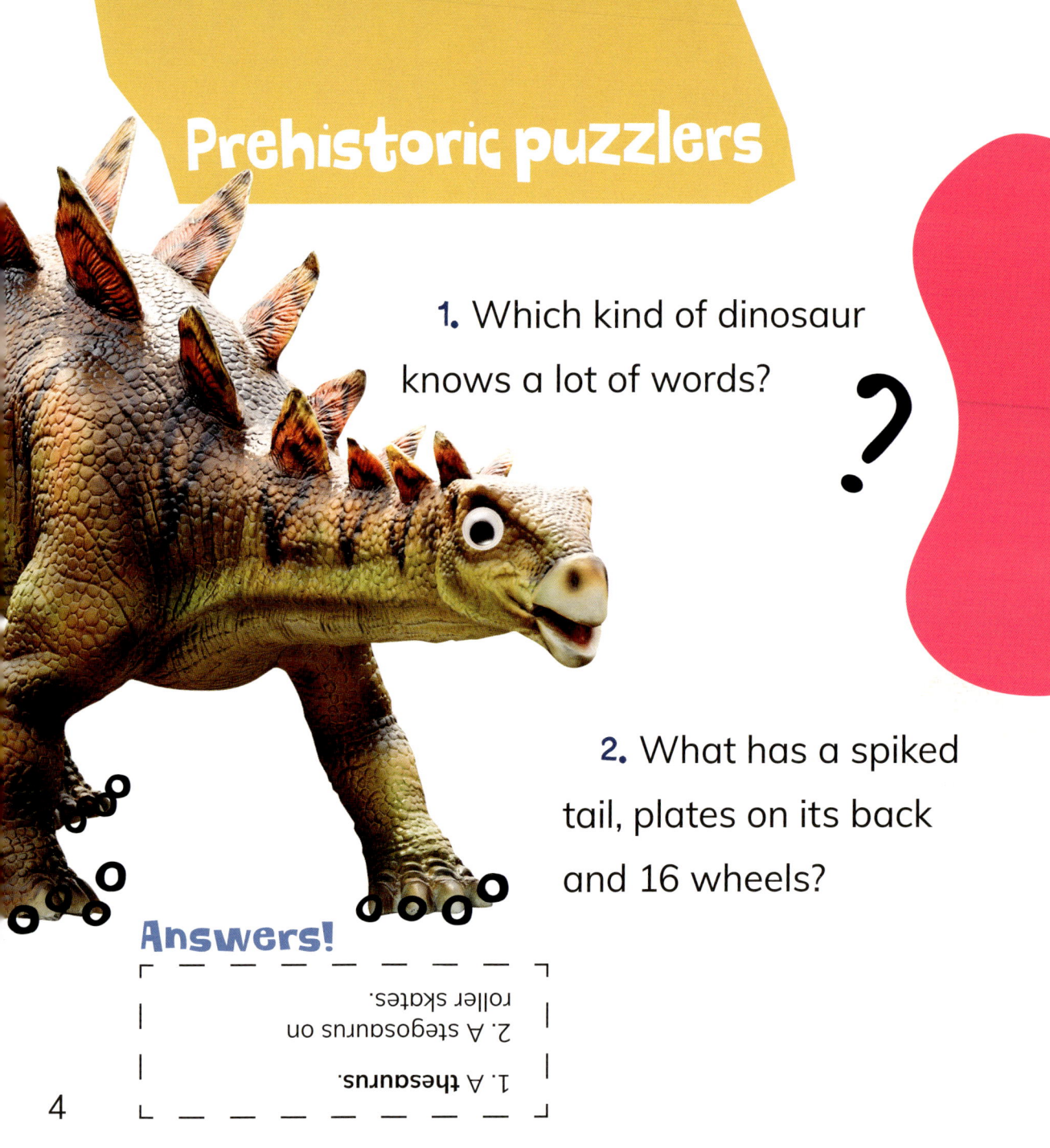

1. Which kind of dinosaur knows a lot of words?

2. What has a spiked tail, plates on its back and 16 wheels?

Answers!

1. A **thesaurus**.
2. A stegosaurus on roller skates.

3. What came after the dinosaur that crossed the road?

4. What's the best way to raise a baby dinosaur?

Answers!
3. Its tail.
4. With an elevator.

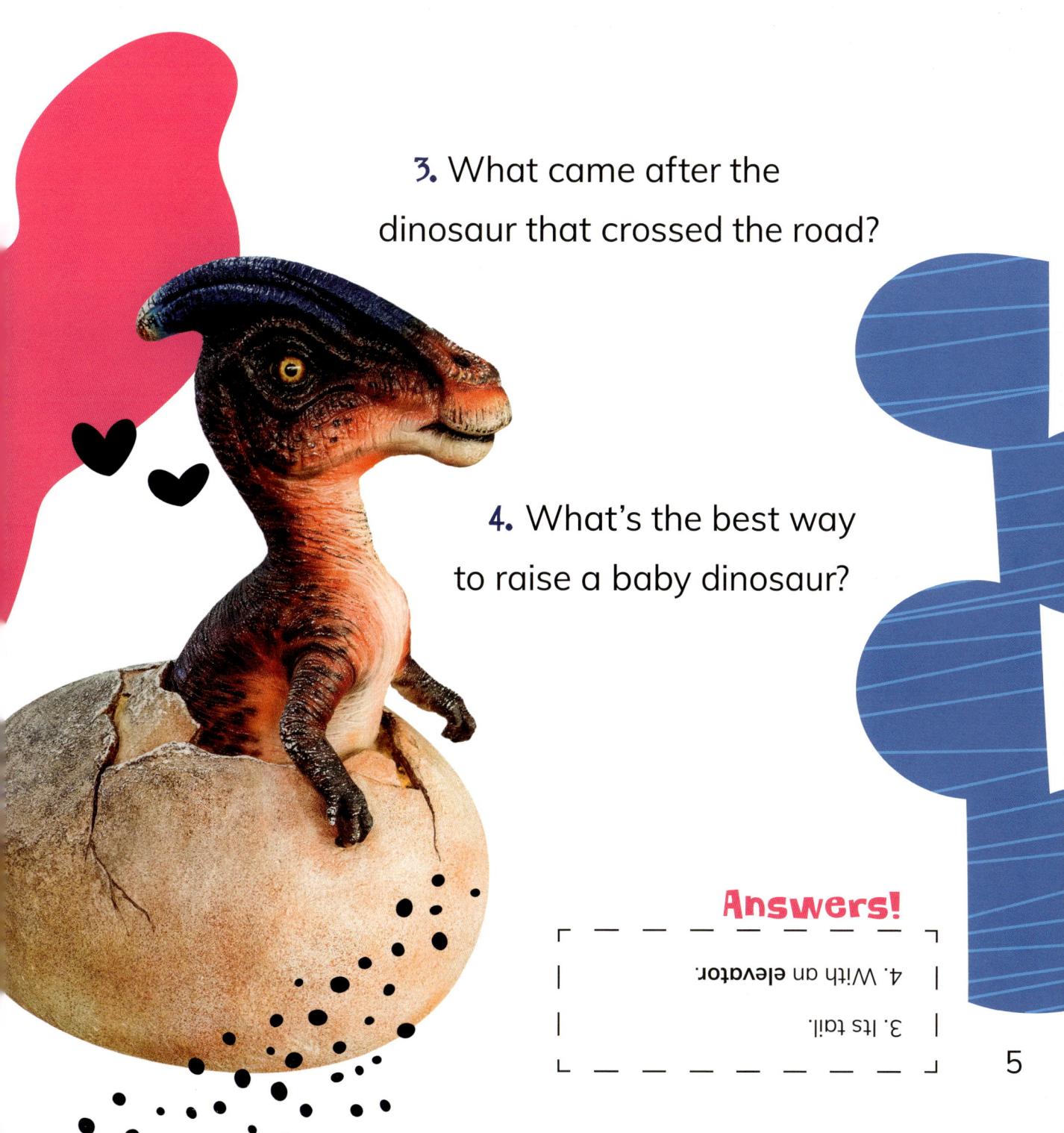

5. Where was the velociraptor when the Sun went down?

6. What do you call an **anxious** dinosaur?

Answers!

5. In the dark.
6. A nervous rex.

7. What happened to the dinosaur that had a bath?

8. Why can't you hear a pterodactyl go to the bathroom?

Answers!

7. It became ex-stinked.
8. Because the "P" is silent.

9. What was the name of the scariest dinosaur?

10. What do you call a dinosaur with no eyes?

Answers!

9. The terror-dactyl.

10. Do-ya-think-he-saurus.

11. What happens when you drop a horned triceratops into the Red Sea?

Answer!

11. It gets wet.

Super Stumpers

12. When can three huge apatosauruses get under a tiny umbrella and not get wet?

Answers!

12. When it's not raining.

13. Which type of dinosaur can jump higher than a house?

14. What do you get when a brontosaurus walks through a strawberry field?

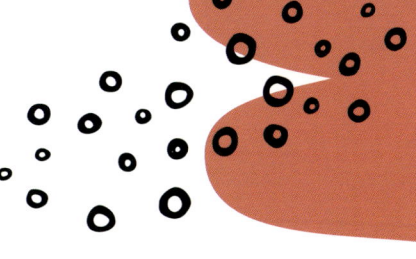

Answers!

13. All of them. Houses can't jump.
14. Strawberry jam.

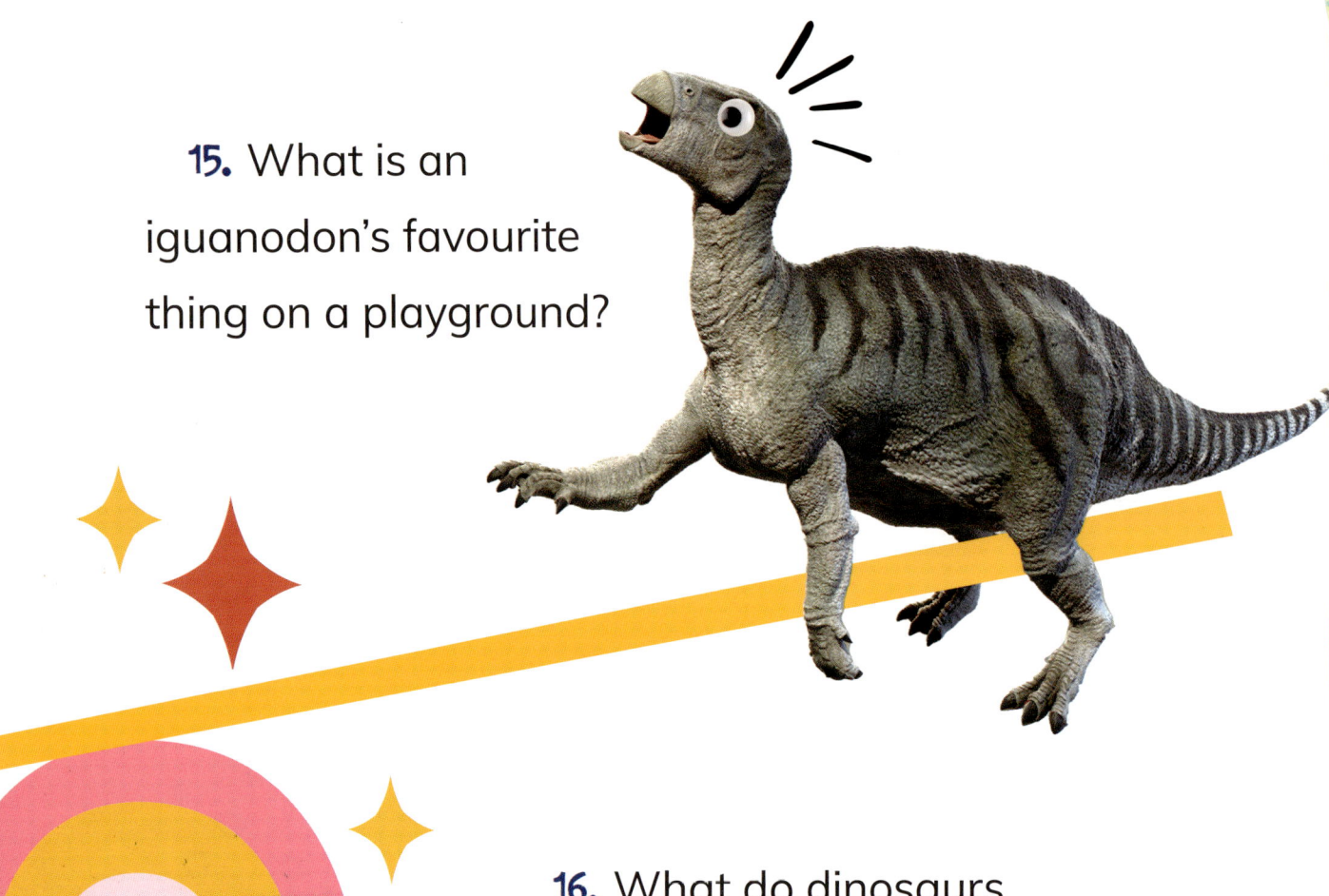

15. What is an iguanodon's favourite thing on a playground?

16. What do dinosaurs use to power their cars?

Answers!

15. The dino-see-saur.
16. **Fossil fuels.**

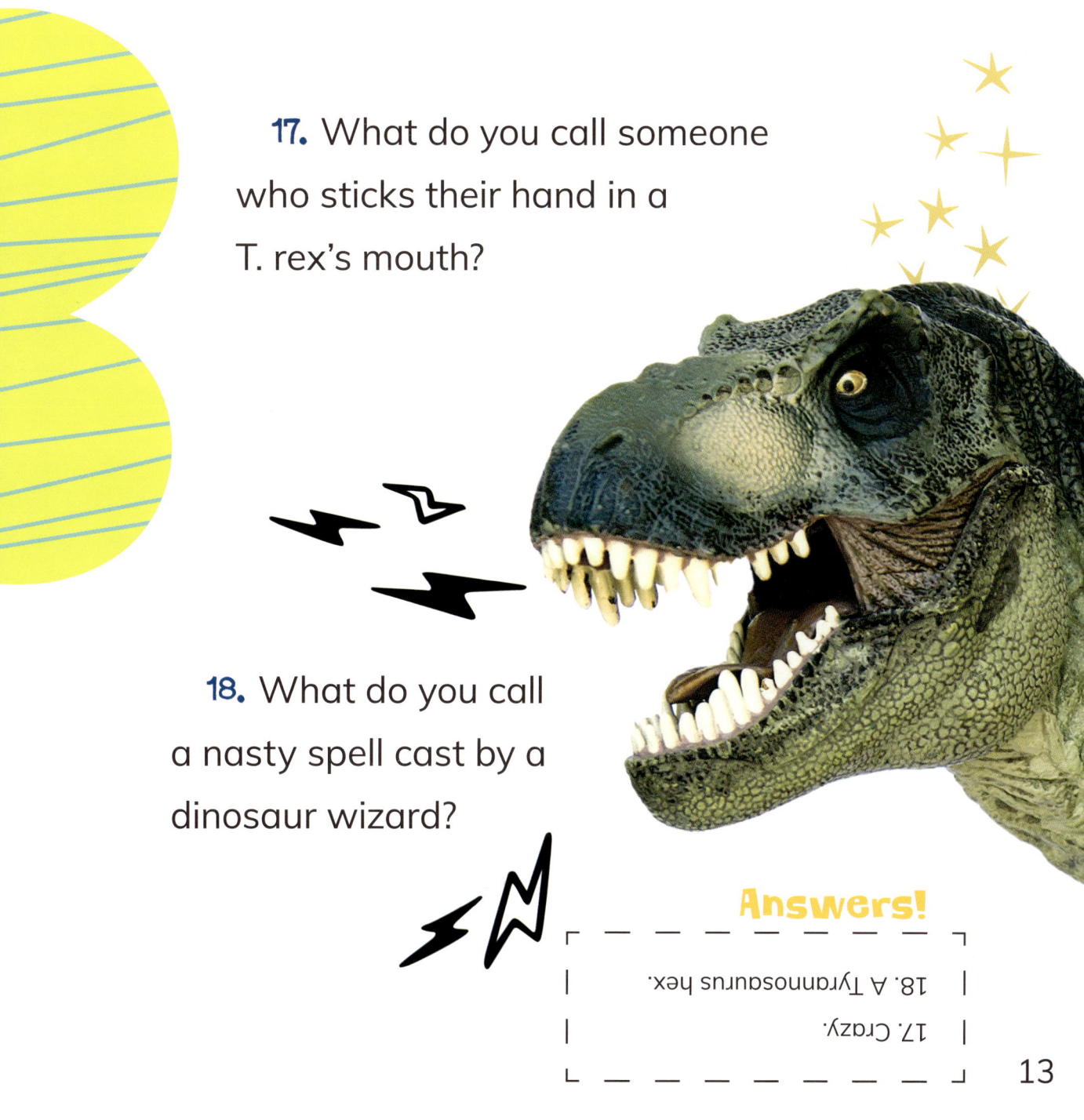

17. What do you call someone who sticks their hand in a T. rex's mouth?

18. What do you call a nasty spell cast by a dinosaur wizard?

Answers!
17. Crazy.
18. A Tyrannosaurus hex.

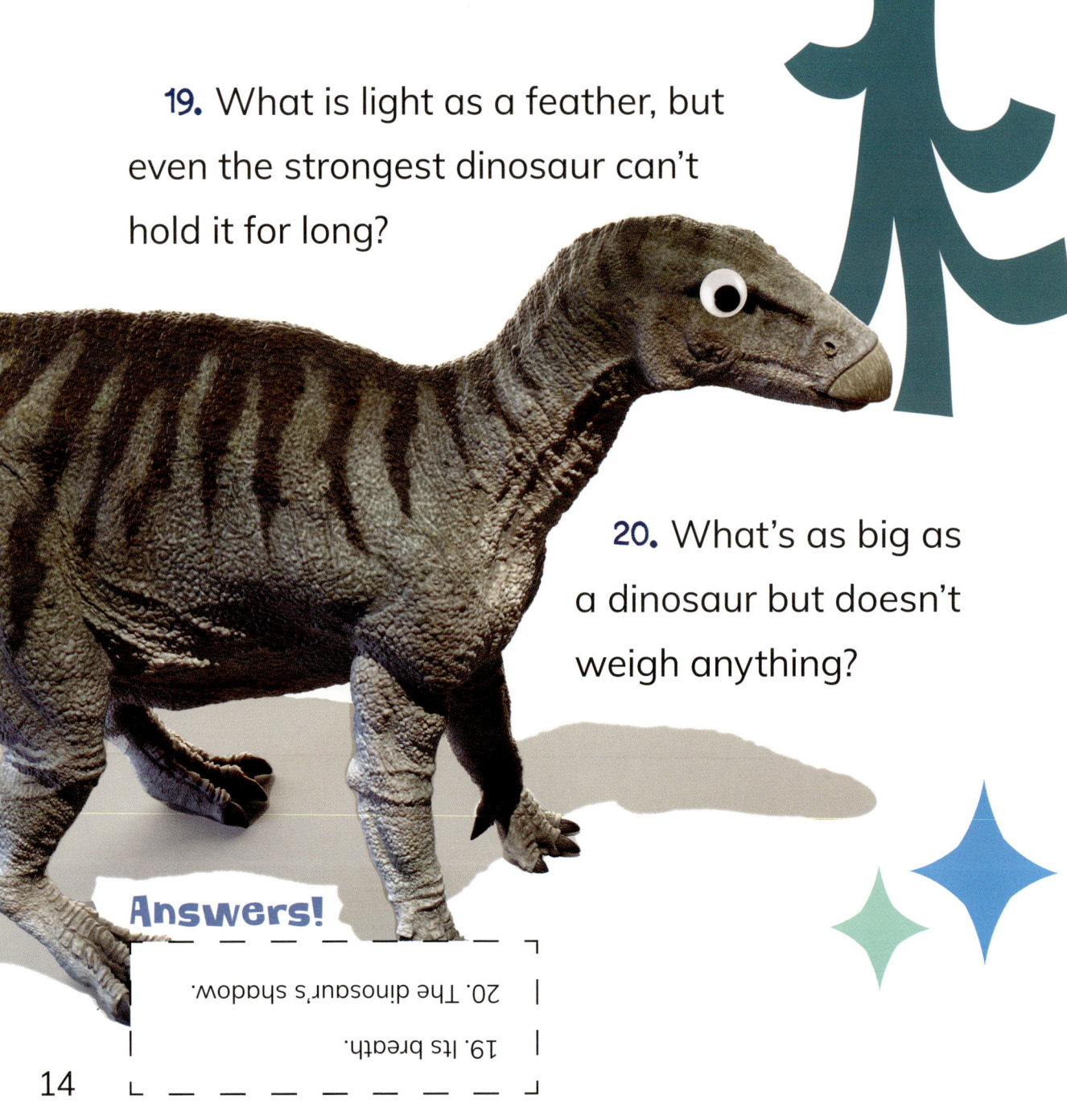

19. What is light as a feather, but even the strongest dinosaur can't hold it for long?

20. What's as big as a dinosaur but doesn't weigh anything?

Answers!

19. Its breath.
20. The dinosaur's shadow.

21. Why did the archaeopteryx (ahr-kee-OP-tuh-riks) catch the worm?

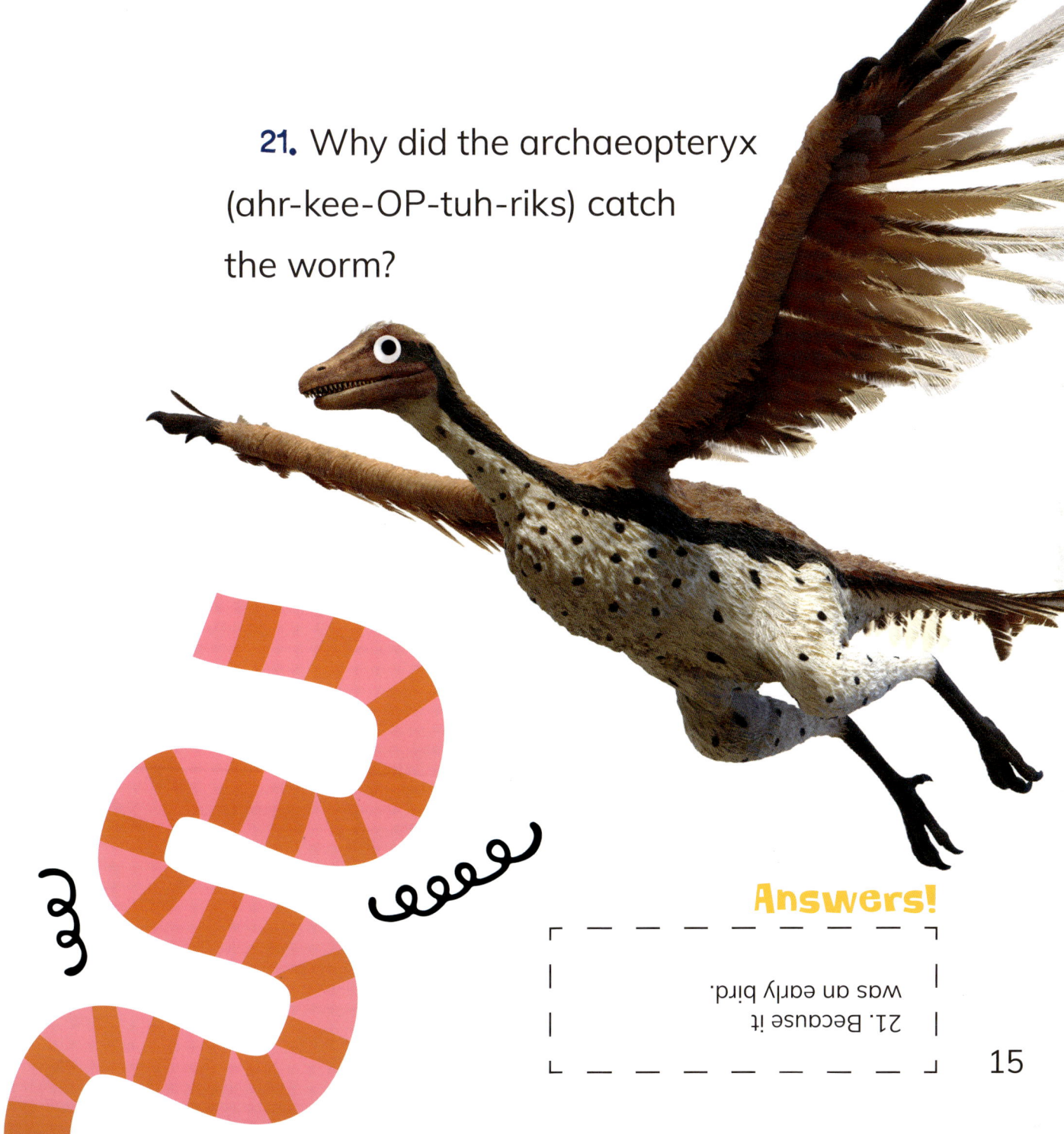

Answers!

21. Because it was an early bird.

Baffling brainteasers

22. Why do museums have old dinosaur bones?

Answers!

22. Because they can't afford new ones.

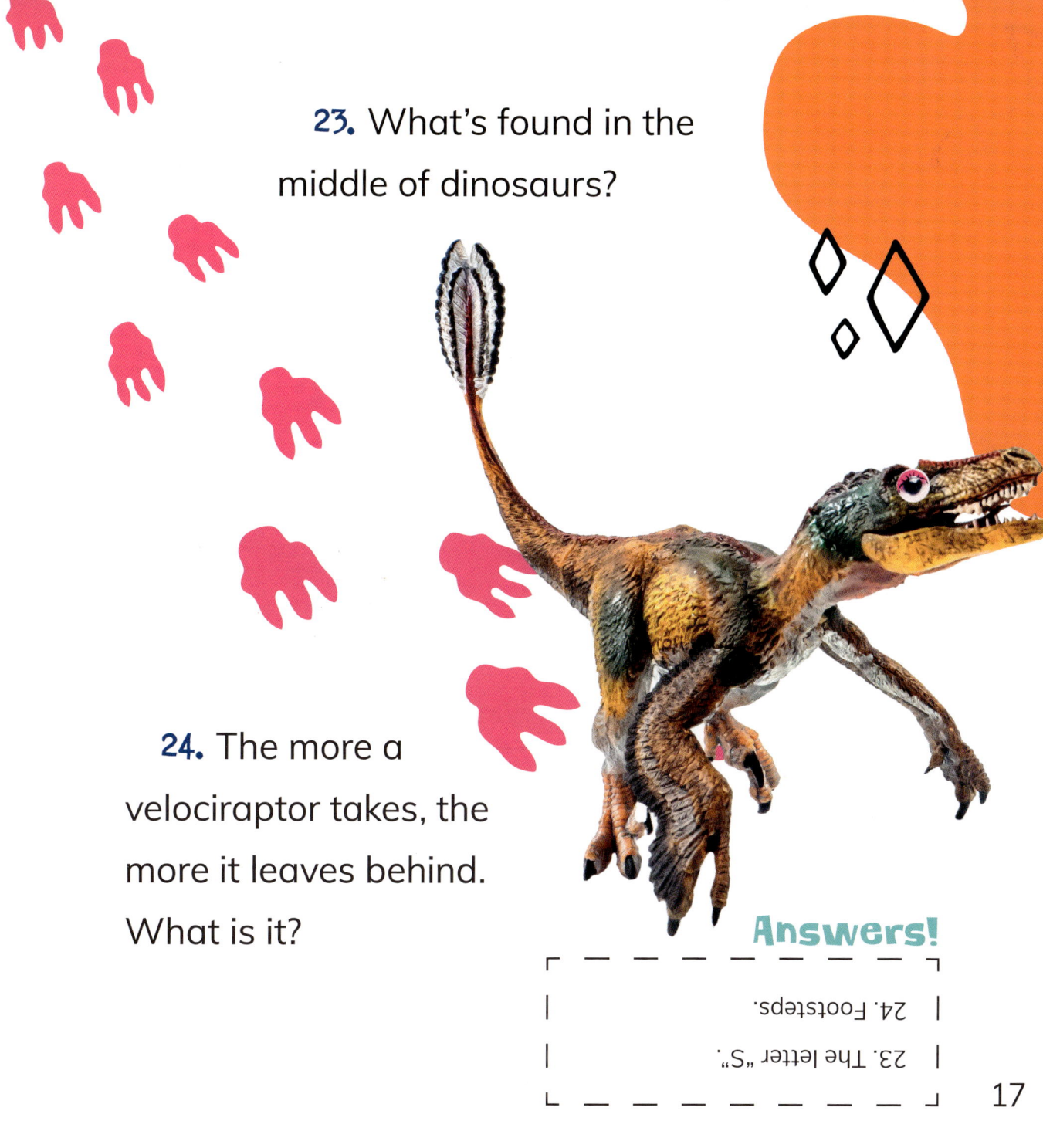

23. What's found in the middle of dinosaurs?

24. The more a velociraptor takes, the more it leaves behind. What is it?

Answers!
23. The letter "S".
24. Footsteps.

25. There are two dinosaurs in front of one dinosaur, two dinosaurs behind another dinosaur, and one dinosaur in the middle. How many dinosaurs are there?

26. What do you get when you cross a pig with a dinosaur?

Answers!

25. Three.
26. Jurassic Pork.

27. What came first: the chicken or the egg?

28. Imagine you're trapped in a room with a **vicious** dinosaur. There are no doors or windows. How do you get out?

Answers!

27. The egg. Dinosaurs laid eggs long before there were chickens.
28. Just stop imagining.

29. If a plane crashes on an island full of hungry dinosaurs, where do you bury the **survivors**?

Answers!

29. Nowhere. You don't bury survivors.

30. How many fish can a megalodon eat on an empty stomach?

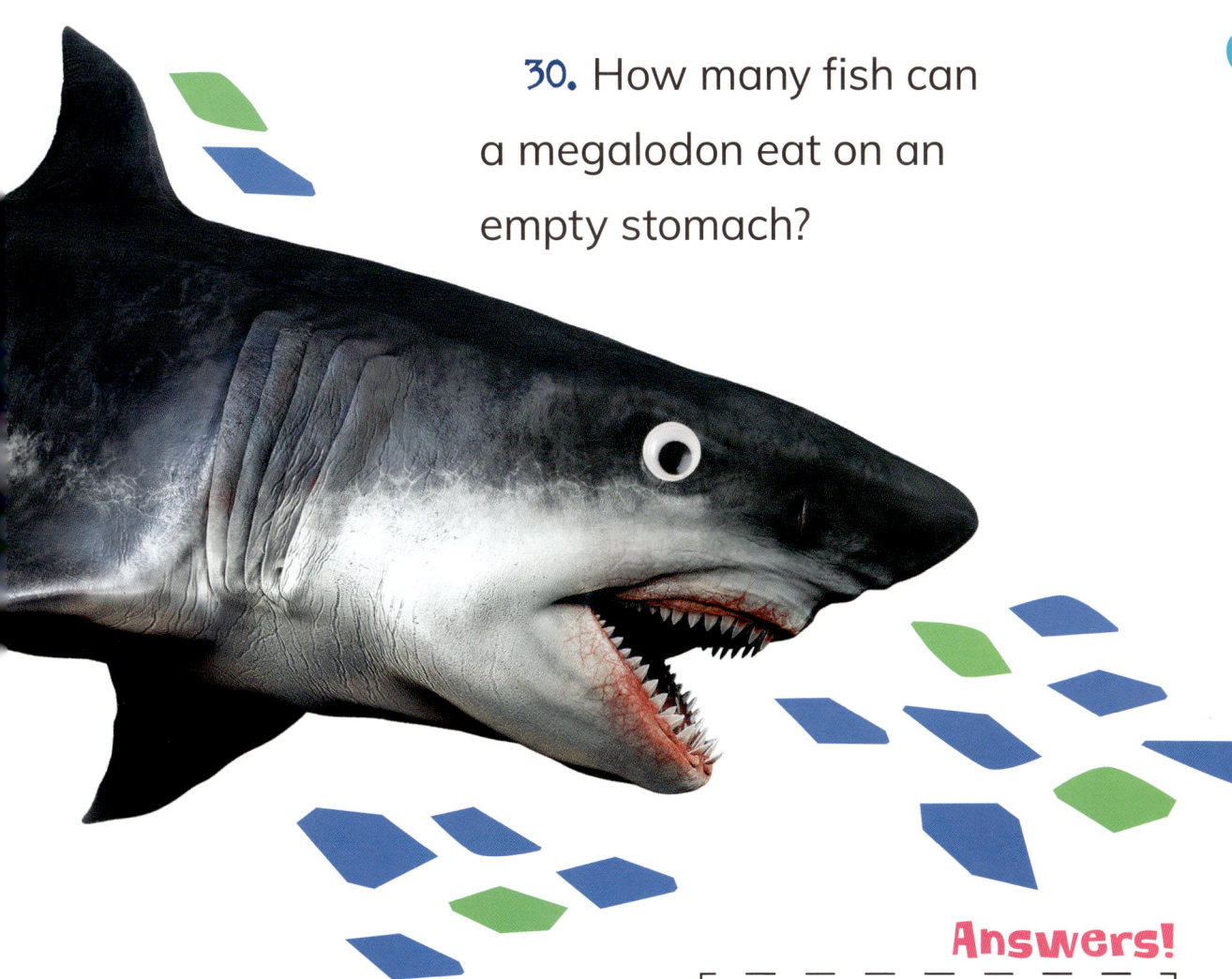

Answers!

30. One. After that, the megalodon's stomach isn't empty.

Glossary

anxious feeling nervous or worried about something

elevator a platform or cage used to lift people or objects from one level to another

fossil fuel natural fuels, such as coal, oil or natural gas, that are formed from the remains of plants and animals

survivor someone who lives through a disaster or a horrible event

thesaurus a book that lists words that are similar to other words

vicious fierce or dangerous

Find out more

Books

Dinosaur Jokes for Funny Kids (Buster Laugh-a-lot Books), Andrew Pinder (Buster Books, 2021)

The Funniest Dinosaur Joke Book Ever, Joe King (Andersen Press, 2018)

Websites

55 Dinosaur Jokes
ponly.com/dinosaur-jokes-puns-riddles/

Dinosaur Jokes and Riddles
enchantedlearning.com/jokes/animals/dinosaur.shtml

Fun Kids Jokes: Dinosaur Jokes
funkidsjokes.com/dinosaur-jokes-for-kids/

Index

apatosaurus 10
archaeopteryx 15

baby dinosaurs 5
bones 16
brontosaurus 11

cars 12
chickens 19

eggs 19
eyes 8

iguanodon 12

jumping 11

megalodon 21

pigs 18
pterodactyl 7

spells 13
stegosaurus 4
survivors 20

T. rex 13
triceratops 9

velociraptor 6, 17

About the author

A. J. Sautter is an author and editor of dozens of kids' books on everything from aliens to zombies. He enjoys reading, going to the cinema and going for long walks with his fluffy, adorable dogs